INTRODUCTION

In the early dawn of World War II, the German military introduced a revolutionary strategy known as "Blitzkrieg," or "lightning war." This tactic emphasized rapid, concentrated attacks to quickly overwhelm and incapacitate the enemy. The success of Blitzkrieg reshaped modern warfare, demonstrating that speed, surprise, and decisive action could topple even the most fortified defenses.

In the fast-paced, competitive world of business, the principles of Blitzkrieg can be just as transformative. Companies today face a battlefield of their own—an ever-changing landscape of market shifts, technological advancements, and consumer demands. To survive and thrive, businesses must adopt strategies that enable them to move quickly, make bold decisions, and seize opportunities before their competitors do.

This book, "Blitzkrieg in Business," will guide you through the principles of this powerful approach and demonstrate how you can apply them to achieve breakthrough success. From startups to established corporations, every organization can benefit from the tactics of speed, surprise, and focused effort.

CHAPTER 1: THE ESSENCE OF BLITZKRIEG

Understanding Blitzkrieg

Blitzkrieg, a term that translates to "lightning war," was a military strategy that changed the course of history. Introduced by the German military in the early days of World War II, it emphasized rapid, concentrated attacks designed to quickly overwhelm and incapacitate the enemy. The strategy was revolutionary, combining speed, surprise, and decisive action to achieve victories that seemed impossible by traditional means.

The core principles of Blitzkrieg were straightforward yet powerful:

1. **Speed**: Swift movement and rapid decision-making to outpace the enemy.
2. **Concentration of Force**: Focusing overwhelming power at critical points to break through enemy lines.
3. **Flexibility**: Adapting to changing situations on the battlefield to maintain the initiative.

These principles allowed the German military to launch sudden, powerful offensives that caught their enemies off guard, leading to quick and decisive victories. The success of Blitzkrieg reshaped modern warfare, proving that speed and agility could overcome even the most fortified defenses.

Translating Military Strategy to Business

In the competitive world of business, companies face a battlefield of their own. Markets are constantly evolving, technology advances at a breakneck pace, and consumer preferences shift rapidly. To succeed, businesses must adopt strategies that enable them to move quickly, make bold decisions, and seize opportunities before their competitors do. The principles of

Blitzkrieg—speed, concentration of force, and flexibility—can be just as effective in the business world as they were on the battlefield.

Speed

In business, speed is crucial in delivering services faster than competitors, rapidly innovating, and swiftly resolving customer issues. Speed means being first to market with new products, services, or innovations, allowing companies to seize market share before rivals can respond. It also involves quick decision-making and execution, enabling businesses to adapt promptly to changes in the market. These facets of speed help a company stay ahead, responding nimbly to evolving market demands.

Concentration of Force

Concentration of force in business involves focusing their limited resources on the most promising opportunities. Just as military strategists concentrate their power at critical points, business leaders must identify high-potential areas and invest heavily in them. This focus ensures that efforts are not diluted and that the company can achieve significant impact where it matters most. It's all about concentrating your resources in the right places, for the maximum possible reward.

Flexibility

Flexibility is the ability to adapt to changing circumstances. In a dynamic market, businesses must be able to pivot their strategies in response to new information, emerging trends, or unforeseen challenges. Flexibility also means fostering a culture of continuous learning and innovation, where experimentation is encouraged and new ideas are constantly being tested.

The Blitzkrieg Mindset

Adopting a Blitzkrieg approach in business requires a fundamental shift in mindset. It means embracing a philosophy of rapid, decisive action and being willing to take risks in pursuit of breakthrough success. The Blitzkrieg mindset involves:

1. **Decisive Leadership**: Leaders must be able to make bold decisions quickly and with confidence. Decisive leadership is crucial for maintaining the speed and momentum necessary for a Blitzkrieg approach.
2. **Empowerment and Trust**: Empowering employees to take initiative and make decisions at all levels of the organization. Trusting your team to act swiftly and effectively is essential for maintaining agility.
3. **Focus on Execution**: Execution is everything. A great strategy is worthless without effective execution. The Blitzkrieg approach emphasizes disciplined, focused execution to achieve rapid results.

Implementing Blitzkrieg in Your Business

To implement the principles of Blitzkrieg in your business, start by assessing your current strategies and identifying areas where speed, concentration of force, and flexibility can be improved. Consider the following steps:

1. **Assess Market Opportunities**: Identify high-potential opportunities in your market where you can achieve significant impact.
2. **Streamline Decision-Making**: Simplify and accelerate your decision-making processes to enable rapid action.
3. **Focus Resources**: Concentrate your resources on the most promising opportunities, ensuring that efforts are not spread too thin.
4. **Foster a Culture of Agility**: Encourage a culture of continuous learning, experimentation, and adaptability within your organization.
5. **Empower Your Team**: Trust and empower your employees to take initiative and make decisions quickly.

By embracing the principles of Blitzkrieg, you can position your business to move swiftly, seize opportunities, and achieve breakthrough success in today's fast-paced, competitive environment. The battle for market leadership is fierce, but with the right strategy, you can emerge victorious.

CHAPTER 2: SPEED – THE NEED FOR SPEED

The Importance of Being First

In today's business environment, speed is not just an advantage—it is a necessity. Companies that can quickly develop and launch new products or services often capture market share before competitors even have a chance to react. Being first to market allows a company to set the standard, shape consumer expectations, and build a loyal customer base. The importance of speed in business cannot be overstated, as it often determines the difference between market leaders and those left struggling to catch up.

Consider the case of Apple with the iPhone. By being the first to bring a truly revolutionary smartphone to the market, Apple set the benchmark for mobile devices and secured a dominant position that competitors are still trying to emulate. This first-mover advantage is a powerful testament to the need for speed in business.

The concept of 'first-mover advantage,' fundamental in game theory, plays a pivotal role in the strategic positioning of businesses. This advantage accrues to companies that are first to enter a market, allowing them to establish strong brand recognition, secure customer loyalty, and accrue significant market share before rivals step in. The benefits extend beyond mere market presence; first movers can set pricing benchmarks, influence customer preferences, and establish high barriers to entry for subsequent competitors. This strategic edge becomes particularly critical in markets characterized by rapid technological change or consumer preference shifts, where being first can translate into long-term competitive supremacy. As such, understanding and harnessing first-mover advantage can be crucial for companies aiming to lead rather than follow in their industries.

Building a Culture of Agility

Creating a fast-moving organization requires more than just quick decision-making; it demands a culture that embraces change and innovation. A culture of agility is one where employees are empowered to take initiative, experiment with new ideas, and respond swiftly to changing circumstances. Here are some strategies to build such a culture:

1. Empower Employees

Empowerment is key to fostering agility. When employees are given the authority to make decisions and take action, they can respond quickly to opportunities and challenges. This means flattening hierarchical structures and decentralizing decision-making processes.

2. Encourage Experimentation

A culture of agility encourages experimentation and innovation. Employees should feel comfortable testing new ideas without fear of failure. Establishing "innovation labs" or dedicated time for creative projects can foster this environment.

3. Streamline Processes

Streamlined processes enable faster execution. Review and simplify workflows to eliminate unnecessary steps and reduce bureaucracy. This might involve adopting agile methodologies, which emphasize iterative development, collaboration, and flexibility.

The Role of Technology

Technology plays a crucial role in enabling speed in business. Leveraging the latest technological advancements can help companies accelerate their operations and improve their responsiveness. Here are some ways technology can enhance speed:

1. Automation

Automating routine tasks can significantly reduce the time required to complete them, freeing up employees to focus on more strategic activities. Automation tools can streamline everything from customer service to supply chain management.

2. Data Analytics

Data analytics provides valuable insights that can inform quick decision-making. By analyzing real-time data, businesses can identify trends, anticipate customer needs, and respond proactively to market changes.

3. Collaboration Tools

Collaboration tools enable teams to communicate and work together more efficiently, regardless of their physical location. Platforms like Slack, Microsoft Teams, and Asana facilitate real-time collaboration, ensuring that projects move forward quickly.

Case Study: Amazon's Obsession with Speed

Amazon is a prime example of a company that has mastered the art of speed. From its inception, Amazon has prioritized quick delivery and fast service. The company's focus on speed is evident in its operations, technology, and culture.

1. Prime Delivery

Amazon Prime's promise of fast, reliable delivery has set a new standard for e-commerce. By investing heavily in logistics and supply chain management, Amazon has made two-day, same-day, and even two-hour delivery possible in many areas.

2. Technological Innovation

Amazon continuously leverages technology to enhance speed. Its use of automation, artificial intelligence, and data analytics ensures that operations are efficient and customer needs are met promptly.

3. Customer-Centric Culture

Amazon's culture is deeply customer-centric, emphasizing the importance of meeting and exceeding customer expectations quickly. This focus drives the company's relentless pursuit of faster delivery times and better service.

Strategies for Speed in Your Business

To achieve speed in your business, consider implementing the following strategies:

1. Set Clear Priorities

Identify the key areas where speed will have the most significant impact and prioritize those areas. This might involve focusing on product development, customer service, or supply chain management.

2. Invest in Technology

Invest in technology that enables speed. This includes automation tools, data analytics platforms, and collaboration software. Ensure that your technology infrastructure supports rapid execution and scalability.

3. Foster a Sense of Urgency

Cultivate a sense of urgency within your organization. Encourage employees to think and act quickly, and reward those who demonstrate initiative and efficiency.

4. Simplify Decision-Making

Simplify decision-making processes to reduce delays. Empower employees at all levels to make decisions and take action without needing excessive approvals.

Measuring and Maintaining Speed

Speed must be measured and maintained to ensure it remains

a priority. Establish key performance indicators (KPIs) that track the speed of your operations, such as time-to-market, order fulfillment times, and customer response times. Regularly review these metrics and make adjustments as needed to maintain high levels of speed.

Chapter Recap

Speed is a critical factor in achieving success in today's fast-paced business environment. By building a culture of agility, leveraging technology, and implementing strategies to enhance speed, businesses can position themselves to outpace competitors and seize market opportunities. The need for speed is not just about being fast; it's about being the first, the best, and the most responsive in a dynamic marketplace. As we continue to explore the principles of Blitzkrieg in business, remember that speed is the foundation upon which rapid, decisive action is built.

CHAPTER 3: CONCENTRATION OF FORCE – FOCUS YOUR EFFORTS

Identifying Your Critical Points

Concentration of force is about focusing your resources on the most critical points where they can have the greatest impact. In business, this means identifying high-potential opportunities and investing heavily in them. This focused effort ensures that your initiatives are not spread too thin, allowing you to achieve significant results in key areas. You and your employees have limited time to give, your organization has limited money to spend. Concentration of force is all about focusing your time and resources on the few opportunities that bring the biggest rewards.

Analyzing Your Business Landscape

To identify these critical points, you need a thorough understanding of your business landscape. This involves:

1. **Market Analysis**: Conduct a detailed market analysis to identify trends, gaps, and emerging opportunities. Look for areas where there is high demand and low competition.
2. **Customer Insights**: Gather insights from your customers to understand their needs, preferences, and pain points. This will help you identify opportunities to create value.
3. **Competitive Analysis**: Analyze your competitors to understand their strengths and weaknesses. Look for areas where you can differentiate yourself and gain a competitive advantage.

Prioritizing Opportunities

Once you have a clear understanding of your business landscape, prioritize the opportunities based on their potential impact and feasibility. Consider factors such as market size, growth potential, alignment with your strengths, and the resources required to pursue them.

Strategic Resource Allocation

Effective concentration of force requires strategic allocation of resources. This means directing your time, money, and talent towards the opportunities with the highest potential for success.

Focusing on Core Competencies

Identify your core competencies—the unique strengths and capabilities that set you apart from competitors. Focus your resources on leveraging these competencies to create value and achieve your business objectives.

Budget Allocation

Allocate your budget strategically to support your prioritized initiatives. Ensure that you have sufficient funding for critical projects and avoid spreading your resources too thin across too many initiatives.

Talent Management

Deploy your top talent to the most critical projects. Ensure that your key employees are working on high-impact initiatives where their skills and expertise can make the greatest difference.

Saying "No" to Distractions

A crucial aspect of concentration of force is the ability to say "no" to distractions and opportunities that do not align with your strategic priorities. This requires discipline and a clear focus on your long-term goals.

Avoiding Opportunity Overload

In a fast-paced business environment, it's easy to get overwhelmed by the sheer number of opportunities available.

However, chasing too many opportunities can dilute your efforts and reduce your effectiveness. Focus on a few high-impact initiatives and execute them with excellence.

Establishing Criteria for Decision-Making

Develop clear criteria for evaluating opportunities and making decisions. This might include factors such as strategic alignment, potential return on investment, and resource requirements. Use these criteria to guide your decisions and ensure that you stay focused on your priorities.

Case Study: Apple's Focus on Core Products

Apple is a prime example of a company that has mastered the art of concentration of force. Despite being one of the largest companies in the world, Apple maintains a relatively small product lineup, focusing its resources on a few high-impact products.

Strategic Product Focus

Apple's focus on a limited number of products allows it to concentrate its resources on innovation, quality, and marketing. By focusing on core products such as the iPhone, iPad, Mac, and Apple Watch, Apple can ensure that each product receives the attention and resources needed to achieve excellence.

Resource Allocation

Apple allocates substantial resources to research and development (R&D) to continuously innovate and improve its products. This focused investment in R&D has led to groundbreaking innovations and maintained Apple's competitive edge.

Discipline in Product Decisions

Apple is known for its discipline in saying "no" to product ideas that do not align with its strategic priorities. This focus enables Apple to maintain a high level of quality and consistency across its product lineup.

Implementing Concentration of Force in Your Startup

To implement concentration of force in your startup, follow these steps:

1. **Identify High-Impact Opportunities**: Conduct market, customer, and competitive analyses to identify the most promising opportunities.
2. **Prioritize Initiatives**: Rank these opportunities based on their potential impact and feasibility. Focus on a few high-impact initiatives.
3. **Allocate Resources Strategically**: Direct your time, money, and talent towards these prioritized initiatives. Ensure that you have sufficient resources to execute them effectively.
4. **Maintain Focus and Discipline**: Avoid distractions and opportunities that do not align with your strategic priorities. Use clear criteria to guide your decision-making.

Tools and Frameworks for Strategic Focus

Several tools and frameworks can help you implement concentration of force in ymour business:

SWOT Analysis

A SWOT analysis helps you identify your strengths, weaknesses, opportunities, and threats. Use this analysis to identify high-impact opportunities that align with your strengths and address your weaknesses.

Pareto Principle (80/20 Rule)

The Pareto Principle states that 80% of your results come from 20% of your efforts. Identify the 20% of activities that drive the most value for your business and focus your resources on these activities.

Balanced Scorecard

The Balanced Scorecard is a strategic planning and management tool that helps you align your business activities with your strategic objectives. Use this tool to track your progress and ensure that your efforts are concentrated on high-impact initiatives.

Chapter Recap

Concentration of force is a powerful principle that can drive significant results in your business. By identifying and prioritizing high-impact opportunities, strategically allocating your resources, and maintaining focus and discipline, you can achieve breakthrough success. The ability to focus your efforts on the most critical points is what separates high-performing companies from the rest. As you continue to implement the principles of Blitzkrieg in your business, remember that concentration of force is about making deliberate, strategic choices and executing them with maximum effort.

CHAPTER 4: FLEXIBILITY – ADAPTING TO CHANGE

The Power of Pivoting

In the dynamic and unpredictable landscape of modern business, the ability to pivot is crucial for survival and success. Pivoting means making a significant change in your strategy, product, or approach in response to new information or changing circumstances. The most successful companies are those that can recognize when a pivot is necessary and execute it effectively.

Recognizing the Need to Pivot

The first step in pivoting is recognizing when a change is necessary. This involves:

1. **Monitoring Performance**: Continuously track key performance indicators (KPIs) to identify areas where your current strategy may be underperforming.
2. **Listening to Customers**: Regularly gather feedback from your customers to understand their needs, preferences, and pain points.
3. **Analyzing Market Trends**: Stay informed about industry trends, competitor movements, and technological advancements that could impact your business.

Types of Pivots

There are several types of pivots that a business might consider:

1. **Product Pivot**: Changing the core product or service offering based on customer feedback or market demand.
2. **Market Pivot**: Targeting a different market segment or demographic that shows greater potential.
3. **Business Model Pivot**: Altering the way you generate

revenue, such as moving from a subscription model to a freemium model.
4. **Technology Pivot**: Adopting new technologies to improve your product or operations.

Continuous Learning and Innovation

Flexibility in business also means fostering a culture of continuous learning and innovation. This involves creating an environment where employees are encouraged to explore new ideas, experiment, and learn from both successes and failures.

Creating a Learning Culture

1. **Encourage Experimentation**: Allow employees to test new ideas without fear of failure. Celebrate both successful innovations and the learning that comes from unsuccessful attempts.
2. **Provide Learning Opportunities**: Offer training programs, workshops, and access to resources that help employees develop new skills and stay updated on industry trends.
3. **Foster Open Communication**: Create channels for open communication and idea sharing within the organization. Encourage collaboration across teams to spark innovation.

Implementing Innovation Processes

1. **Innovation Labs**: Set up dedicated innovation labs where employees can work on experimental projects without the constraints of day-to-day operations.
2. **Hackathons and Workshops**: Organize hackathons and innovation workshops to generate new ideas and solutions.
3. **Customer Co-Creation**: Involve customers in the innovation process by seeking their input on new product features and improvements.

Building Agile Teams

Agile teams are essential for maintaining flexibility and adaptability in a fast-paced business environment. Agile methodologies, such as Scrum and Kanban, provide frameworks for teams to work efficiently and respond quickly to changes.

Principles of Agile Teams

1. **Cross-Functional Collaboration**: Agile teams are cross-functional, bringing together members with diverse skills to work collaboratively on projects.
2. **Iterative Development**: Work is divided into short cycles or sprints, allowing teams to develop, test, and refine products incrementally.
3. **Continuous Feedback**: Agile teams prioritize regular feedback from customers and stakeholders to ensure that the product meets their needs and expectations.

Implementing Agile Methodologies

1. **Scrum**: Scrum involves dividing work into sprints, with each sprint typically lasting 2-4 weeks. Teams hold daily stand-up meetings to discuss progress and plan next steps. At the end of each sprint, a review meeting is held to assess the results and gather feedback.
2. **Kanban**: Kanban focuses on visualizing work, limiting work in progress, and improving flow. Tasks are represented on a Kanban board, which helps teams track progress and identify bottlenecks.

Adapting to Market Changes

In a rapidly changing market, the ability to adapt quickly can be a significant competitive advantage. This involves staying attuned to market signals and being ready to adjust your strategy as needed.

Market Intelligence

1. **Regular Market Analysis**: Conduct regular market analysis to stay informed about trends, emerging technologies, and shifts in consumer behavior.
2. **Competitive Intelligence**: Monitor your competitors' activities to identify opportunities and threats. Use this information to adjust your strategy and stay ahead of the competition.

Responsive Strategy

1. **Flexible Planning**: Adopt a flexible approach to strategic planning. Instead of rigid, long-term plans, focus on short-term goals and regularly review and adjust your strategy based on new information.
2. **Scenario Planning**: Use scenario planning to anticipate potential future scenarios and develop contingency plans. This prepares your business to respond quickly to unexpected changes.

Case Study: Netflix's Pivot to Streaming

Netflix provides a powerful example of flexibility and the ability to pivot successfully. Originally a DVD rental service, Netflix recognized the potential of streaming technology and shifted its business model to become a leading streaming service.

Recognizing the Need to Pivot

In the early 2000s, Netflix observed the rapid growth of internet bandwidth and the increasing demand for on-demand entertainment. This market insight prompted Netflix to pivot from its DVD rental model to streaming.

Implementing the Pivot

Netflix invested heavily in streaming technology and content acquisition. They developed a user-friendly streaming platform and began producing original content to differentiate themselves from competitors.

Results

The pivot to streaming transformed Netflix into a global entertainment powerhouse, with millions of subscribers worldwide and a market-leading position in the industry.

Implementing Flexibility in Your Startup

To implement flexibility in your startup, follow these steps:

1. **Foster a Learning Culture**: Encourage experimentation, provide learning opportunities, and foster open communication.
2. **Build Agile Teams**: Implement agile methodologies to enable efficient and responsive teamwork.
3. **Stay Informed**: Conduct regular market and competitive analysis to stay attuned to changes and opportunities.
4. **Be Ready to Pivot**: Recognize when a pivot is necessary and be prepared to make significant changes to your strategy or product.
5. **Develop Flexible Plans**: Focus on short-term goals and regularly review and adjust your strategy based on new information.

Chapter Recap

Flexibility is a crucial principle for achieving success in today's fast-paced business environment. By fostering a culture of continuous learning and innovation, building agile teams, and staying attuned to market changes, your startup can adapt quickly and effectively to new challenges and opportunities. The ability to pivot and maintain flexibility will position your business for long-term success, allowing you to navigate the complexities of the market and stay ahead of the competition. As you continue to implement the principles of Blitzkrieg in your business, remember that flexibility is about being proactive, responsive, and ready to change course when necessary.

CHAPTER 5: RECRUITMENT – BUILDING A HIGH-PERFORMING TEAM

We've emphasized the importance of empowering employees to make decisions and delegating decision-making processes to avoid an overly bureaucratic organization that stifles action. However, the foundation of this empowerment and delegation lies in recruiting highly competent employees. The value of a business is fundamentally rooted in its people; the competency of individuals at all levels can make or break a business. Incompetent employees can be costly and hard to manage, making it essential to focus on recruitment practices that ensure you build a high-performing team.

The Importance of Competent Employees

1. **Efficiency and Productivity**: Competent employees perform tasks more efficiently, reducing the time and resources needed to achieve business goals. Their productivity directly impacts the company's bottom line.
2. **Innovation and Creativity**: High-performing employees bring innovative ideas and creative solutions to the table, driving the company forward and helping it stay competitive in a rapidly changing market.
3. **Decision-Making and Problem-Solving**: Skilled employees make better decisions and solve problems more effectively, contributing to the overall agility and responsiveness of the organization.
4. **Culture and Morale**: Competent employees contribute positively to the company culture and morale, creating a motivating and engaging work environment that attracts and retains top talent.

Recruitment Strategies for High Competence

1. Define Your Ideal Candidate Profile

Before you start the recruitment process, clearly define the ideal candidate profile for each position. This profile should include:

- **Technical Skills**: Specific skills and knowledge required for the job.
- **Experience**: Relevant work experience and achievements in similar roles.
- **Soft Skills**: Interpersonal skills, communication abilities, and cultural fit.
- **Values and Attitudes**: Alignment with the company's core values and attitudes towards work and collaboration.

2. Utilize Multiple Recruitment Channels

Use a variety of recruitment channels to reach a diverse pool of candidates:

- **Job Boards and Websites**: Post job listings on popular job boards and industry-specific websites.
- **Social Media**: Leverage platforms like LinkedIn, Twitter, and Facebook to reach potential candidates.
- **Recruitment Agencies**: Partner with recruitment agencies that specialize in your industry to find qualified candidates.
- **Employee Referrals**: Encourage current employees to refer candidates. Employee referrals often result in high-quality hires.

3. Implement a Rigorous Selection Process

A thorough selection process helps ensure that you hire the right candidates:

- **Initial Screening**: Conduct initial screenings to filter out candidates who do not meet the basic requirements.
- **Structured Interviews**: Use structured interviews with standardized questions to assess candidates' competencies and fit.

- **Technical Assessments**: Administer technical tests or practical assignments to evaluate candidates' skills.
- **Behavioral Assessments**: Use behavioral interview questions to understand how candidates have handled past situations and how they align with your company culture.

4. Focus on Cultural Fit

Cultural fit is crucial for long-term success and employee satisfaction:

- **Values Alignment**: Assess whether candidates' values align with the company's core values.
- **Team Compatibility**: Evaluate how well candidates will integrate with existing teams and contribute to a positive work environment.
- **Adaptability**: Look for candidates who are adaptable and open to change, as they will be more likely to thrive in a dynamic business environment.

5. Offer Competitive Compensation and Benefits

Attracting top talent requires offering competitive compensation and benefits:

- **Salary and Bonuses**: Ensure that your salary and bonus structures are competitive within your industry.
- **Benefits**: Offer comprehensive benefits packages, including health insurance, retirement plans, and paid time off.
- **Work-Life Balance**: Promote a healthy work-life balance through flexible work arrangements, remote work options, and wellness programs.

Onboarding and Integration

Once you've recruited highly competent employees, the next step is to onboard and integrate them effectively:

1. Structured Onboarding Program

Develop a structured onboarding program to help new hires

acclimate quickly:

- **Orientation**: Provide an overview of the company, its mission, values, and culture.
- **Role-Specific Training**: Offer training specific to the new hire's role, including tools, processes, and expectations.
- **Mentorship**: Assign mentors or buddies to guide new hires through their initial weeks and months.

2. Clear Goals and Expectations

Set clear goals and expectations from the start:

- **Performance Metrics**: Define key performance indicators (KPIs) and milestones for the new hire.
- **Feedback Mechanisms**: Establish regular feedback mechanisms to provide guidance and support.

3. Foster Engagement and Inclusion

Ensure that new hires feel engaged and included:

- **Team Integration**: Facilitate opportunities for new hires to interact with their team and other departments.
- **Company Events**: Involve new hires in company events and activities to help them feel part of the organization.
- **Open Communication**: Encourage open communication and provide channels for new hires to voice their ideas and concerns.

Continuous Development and Retention

To maintain a high-performing team, focus on continuous development and retention:

1. Professional Development

Invest in the professional development of your employees:

- **Training Programs**: Offer ongoing training programs and workshops to enhance skills and knowledge.
- **Career Pathing**: Provide clear career paths and opportunities

for advancement within the company.
- **Educational Support**: Support further education and certifications through tuition reimbursement or sponsorship programs.

2. Performance Management

Implement effective performance management practices:

- **Regular Reviews**: Conduct regular performance reviews to assess progress and provide feedback.
- **Recognition and Rewards**: Recognize and reward outstanding performance through bonuses, promotions, and public acknowledgment.
- **Improvement Plans**: Develop improvement plans for employees who may need additional support to meet expectations.

3. Employee Engagement

Keep employees engaged and motivated:

- **Work-Life Balance**: Promote work-life balance through flexible scheduling and remote work options.
- **Inclusive Culture**: Foster an inclusive culture where all employees feel valued and respected.
- **Open Communication**: Maintain open lines of communication and involve employees in decision-making processes.

Case Study: Google's Recruitment Excellence

Google is renowned for its rigorous recruitment process and focus on hiring highly competent employees:

Recruitment Strategies

1. **Defined Candidate Profile**: Google clearly defines the ideal candidate profile, emphasizing technical skills, innovation, and cultural fit.
2. **Multiple Channels**: Google utilizes various recruitment

channels, including job boards, social media, and employee referrals.
3. **Selection Process**: Google's selection process includes initial screenings, structured interviews, technical assessments, and behavioral evaluations.

Onboarding and Development

1. **Structured Onboarding**: Google provides a comprehensive onboarding program that includes orientation, role-specific training, and mentorship.
2. **Continuous Development**: Google invests in continuous development through training programs, career pathing, and educational support.

Chapter Recap

Recruiting highly competent employees is the foundation of building a high-performing team and a successful business. By defining the ideal candidate profile, utilizing multiple recruitment channels, implementing a rigorous selection process, and focusing on cultural fit, you can attract and hire top talent. Effective onboarding, continuous development, and retention strategies ensure that your employees remain engaged, motivated, and aligned with your business goals. As you continue to implement the principles of Blitzkrieg in your business, remember that the value of your business is in your people—their competency at all levels will ultimately determine your success.

CHAPTER 6: BALANCING SPEED AND VALUE – AVOIDING THE PITFALLS OF RAPID EXECUTION

In our exploration of the Blitzkrieg approach to business, we have emphasized the importance of speed in achieving competitive advantage. However, an increased sense of urgency can sometimes lead to cutting corners or neglecting the fundamental principle of value creation. Business is fundamentally about delivering value to customers, and if this is compromised in the rush to execute quickly, the company risks failure. The challenge lies in balancing speed with the imperative to create and deliver value as efficiently as possible.

The Importance of Value Creation

1. **Customer Satisfaction**: Delivering value ensures that customers are satisfied with your products or services, leading to repeat business, loyalty, and positive word-of-mouth.
2. **Competitive Advantage**: Value creation differentiates your offerings from competitors, making it easier to attract and retain customers.
3. **Long-Term Success**: Sustainable business growth is built on a foundation of value. Products or services that consistently deliver value can weather market fluctuations and changes in consumer preferences.

The Risks of Neglecting Value

1. **Customer Dissatisfaction**: If a product or service does not meet customer expectations, it can lead to dissatisfaction, negative reviews, and loss of business.
2. **Brand Damage**: Cutting corners can damage your brand's reputation, making it difficult to regain customer trust and market position.

3. **Operational Inefficiencies**: Short-term fixes and rushed executions can lead to long-term operational inefficiencies, requiring costly corrections later on.

Strategies for Balancing Speed and Value

1. Prioritize Core Features and Functionality

When developing a product under time constraints, it's crucial to prioritize core features and functionality that deliver the most value to customers. This ensures that even a minimum viable product (MVP) meets essential customer needs and provides a solid foundation for future improvements.

- **Identify Key Value Drivers**: Determine the key features and functionalities that drive the most value for customers. Focus your development efforts on these areas.
- **Iterative Development**: Use iterative development cycles to release a basic, functional version of the product quickly, then continuously improve it based on user feedback.

2. Implement Robust Quality Assurance

Quality assurance (QA) should never be compromised in the pursuit of speed. Implementing robust QA processes ensures that the product meets high standards of quality, reliability, and performance.

- **Automated Testing**: Use automated testing tools to quickly identify and fix bugs without slowing down the development process.
- **User Testing**: Involve real users in testing to gather feedback and ensure that the product meets their needs and expectations.

3. Foster a Culture of Excellence

Creating a culture that values excellence and quality helps ensure that speed does not come at the expense of value. This involves setting high standards and encouraging employees to strive for excellence in all aspects of their work.

- **Set Clear Expectations**: Clearly communicate the importance of quality and value to all employees. Ensure that everyone understands the company's commitment to delivering high-value products.
- **Reward Quality Work**: Recognize and reward employees who demonstrate a commitment to quality and excellence. This reinforces the importance of value creation within the organization.

4. Efficient Resource Allocation

Efficient resource allocation ensures that projects have the necessary time, budget, and personnel to deliver high-value products without unnecessary delays.

- **Balanced Workloads**: Ensure that workloads are balanced to prevent burnout and maintain high-quality output.
- **Resource Prioritization**: Allocate resources to projects that have the highest potential to deliver significant value to customers.

5. Continuous Improvement and Feedback Loops

Establishing continuous improvement processes and feedback loops helps maintain a focus on value while allowing for rapid iteration and improvement.

- **Regular Reviews**: Conduct regular reviews of products and services to identify areas for improvement and ensure they continue to meet customer needs.
- **Customer Feedback**: Actively seek and incorporate customer feedback to refine and enhance products, ensuring that they deliver maximum value.

Case Study: Tesla's Balancing Act

Tesla, under the leadership of Elon Musk, exemplifies the balance between speed and value. The company is known for its rapid innovation and quick market entries but also maintains a strong focus on delivering high-value products.

Rapid Innovation with Value

- **Innovation**: Tesla continually pushes the boundaries of automotive technology, from electric vehicles to autonomous driving.
- **Quality Assurance**: Despite its rapid pace, Tesla implements rigorous quality assurance processes to ensure that its vehicles meet high standards of safety and performance.
- **Customer-Centric Design**: Tesla's vehicles are designed with a deep understanding of customer needs, ensuring that they deliver significant value in terms of performance, efficiency, and user experience.

Continuous Feedback and Improvement

- **Over-the-Air Updates**: Tesla's ability to provide over-the-air updates allows the company to continuously improve its vehicles based on user feedback and new technological advancements.
- **Customer Engagement**: Tesla engages with its customer base through direct communication, social media, and feedback mechanisms, ensuring that customer needs are always at the forefront of its development efforts.

Implementing the Balance in Your Startup

To implement the balance between speed and value in your startup, consider the following steps:

1. **Define Core Value Proposition**: Clearly define what value your product or service provides to customers and ensure that this is the focal point of your development efforts.
2. **Adopt Agile Methodologies**: Use agile methodologies to iterate quickly while maintaining a focus on quality and customer feedback.

3. **Invest in Quality Assurance**: Allocate resources to robust QA processes to ensure that products meet high standards of quality and reliability.
4. **Encourage a Quality-First Culture**: Foster a culture that values quality and excellence, ensuring that employees understand the importance of delivering value.
5. **Establish Continuous Feedback Loops**: Implement processes for regularly gathering and acting on customer feedback to continuously improve your product.

Chapter Recap

Balancing speed and value is crucial for the long-term success of any business. While rapid execution is important for staying competitive, it should never come at the expense of delivering value to customers. By prioritizing core features, implementing robust quality assurance, fostering a culture of excellence, efficiently allocating resources, and establishing continuous improvement processes, your business can achieve the perfect balance. This ensures that you not only move quickly but also create and deliver products that meet customer needs and drive long-term success. As you continue to implement the principles of Blitzkrieg in your business, remember that true speed is achieved not just by moving quickly, but by moving quickly while delivering exceptional value.

CHAPTER 7: THE POWER OF THE MINIMUM VIABLE PRODUCT (MVP)

In the fast-paced world of business, launching a product quickly while ensuring it delivers significant value is a delicate balance. A powerful strategy to achieve this balance is developing a Minimum Viable Product (MVP). An MVP allows businesses to launch a product with just enough features to satisfy early adopters and provide feedback for future development. By focusing on speed, value, efficiency, and concentration of force, an MVP can be the key to successful product launches and long-term business growth.

Understanding the MVP Concept

An MVP is a version of a new product that includes only the essential features required to address the core problem and provide value to users. The goal is to launch quickly, gather user feedback, and iterate based on real-world data. This approach minimizes the risks associated with lengthy development cycles and ensures that the product evolves in line with customer needs.

The Benefits of an MVP

1. **Speed to Market**: An MVP allows you to launch quickly, capturing market opportunities before competitors do.
2. **Validated Learning**: Early user feedback helps validate assumptions and guides future development.
3. **Resource Efficiency**: By focusing only on essential features, you conserve resources and avoid wasting time and money on unnecessary functionalities.
4. **Risk Mitigation**: Testing the product in the market with a smaller investment reduces the risk of failure.
5. **Customer Engagement**: Engaging early adopters helps build a loyal user base and creates advocates for your

product.

Principles for Developing an MVP

1. Focus on Core Features

Identify the essential features that solve the primary problem your product addresses. These core features should deliver significant value to early adopters.

- **Value Proposition**: Clearly define the value proposition of your MVP. What problem does it solve? How does it benefit users?
- **Feature Prioritization**: Prioritize features based on their importance to the value proposition. Use frameworks like the MoSCoW method (Must have, Should have, Could have, Won't have) to make decisions.

2. Concentration of Force

Allocate your resources strategically to develop and launch the MVP efficiently.

- **Resource Allocation**: Focus your best talent and resources on developing the MVP. This ensures that the essential features are built to a high standard.
- **Cross-Functional Teams**: Form cross-functional teams that include developers, designers, marketers, and product managers. This collaborative approach ensures that all aspects of the product are considered and addressed.

3. Speed and Efficiency

Adopt agile methodologies to ensure rapid development and continuous iteration.

- **Agile Development**: Use agile frameworks like Scrum or Kanban to manage the development process. Break down the project into manageable sprints or tasks, allowing for quick progress and regular reassessment.
- **Iterative Process**: Develop the MVP iteratively, releasing new

versions based on user feedback and performance data. This approach ensures that the product evolves in line with user needs.

4. Gathering and Analyzing Feedback

Engage with early adopters to gather valuable feedback and insights.

- **User Testing**: Conduct user testing sessions to observe how users interact with the MVP. Identify pain points and areas for improvement.
- **Surveys and Interviews**: Use surveys and interviews to gather qualitative feedback from users. Ask open-ended questions to understand their experiences and expectations.
- **Analytics**: Implement analytics tools to track user behavior and gather quantitative data. Analyze metrics like usage frequency, feature engagement, and drop-off points.

Case Study: Dropbox's MVP Approach

Dropbox, the cloud storage service, is a classic example of a successful MVP launch. When Dropbox started, the founders faced skepticism about the viability of their product. Instead of building a fully-featured product, they created a simple video demonstrating the core functionality.

The MVP Process

1. **Identifying Core Features**: Dropbox focused on its core feature—easy file synchronization across devices.
2. **Concentration of Force**: The team concentrated their efforts on developing a seamless, user-friendly experience for this feature.
3. **Speed and Efficiency**: By creating a simple video MVP, Dropbox quickly validated its concept without extensive development.
4. **Gathering Feedback**: The video generated significant interest and feedback, allowing the team to refine their

approach before building the full product.

Results

The Dropbox MVP video attracted thousands of early adopters and validated the market demand. This initial validation provided the confidence and insights needed to develop the full product, leading to Dropbox's success as a leading cloud storage provider.

Implementing an MVP in Your Startup

To implement an MVP in your startup, follow these steps:

1. **Define the Problem and Value Proposition**: Clearly articulate the problem your product solves and the value it provides to users. This will guide feature prioritization and development.
2. **Identify Core Features**: Determine the essential features needed to deliver the core value proposition. Prioritize these features for the MVP.
3. **Assemble a Cross-Functional Team**: Form a team with diverse skills and perspectives to collaborate on the MVP development.
4. **Adopt Agile Methodologies**: Use agile frameworks to manage the development process, ensuring rapid progress and flexibility to adapt based on feedback.
5. **Launch Quickly and Gather Feedback**: Launch the MVP as soon as the core features are ready. Engage with early adopters to gather feedback and analyze data.
6. **Iterate and Improve**: Use the feedback and data to iterate on the product, adding new features and refining existing ones based on user needs.

Balancing Speed and Value in an MVP

Balancing speed and value in an MVP requires careful planning and execution. Here are some tips to maintain this balance:

- **Set Clear Objectives**: Define clear, measurable objectives

for the MVP. These objectives should align with your overall business goals and guide the development process.
- **Maintain Quality**: While speed is important, ensure that the core features are developed to a high standard. Cutting corners on quality can undermine the value of the MVP and damage your brand reputation.
- **Engage with Users**: Maintain close communication with early adopters throughout the MVP phase. Their feedback is invaluable for refining the product and ensuring it delivers the desired value.
- **Be Prepared to Pivot**: If feedback indicates that the MVP is not meeting user needs, be prepared to pivot. This might involve changing features, targeting a different market segment, or even rethinking the value proposition.

Chapter Recap

The Minimum Viable Product (MVP) is a powerful tool for launching products quickly while ensuring they deliver significant value. By focusing on core features, concentrating resources, adopting agile methodologies, and engaging with users, businesses can achieve the perfect balance between speed and value. The MVP approach minimizes risks, conserves resources, and ensures that the product evolves based on real-world feedback. As you continue to implement the principles of Blitzkrieg in your business, remember that the MVP is a strategic weapon that allows you to move quickly, deliver value efficiently, and build a foundation for long-term success.

CHAPTER 8: SCALING OPERATIONS EFFICIENTLY

Scaling operations is a critical phase in the growth of any business. It involves expanding the capacity to handle increased demand while maintaining the quality and efficiency of products or services. Efficient scaling requires strategic planning, a scalable infrastructure, robust processes, and the right talent to support growth. In this chapter, we will explore strategies to scale operations effectively, ensuring that your business can grow sustainably and continue to deliver value to customers.

The Importance of Scalable Infrastructure

A scalable infrastructure is the backbone of any growing business. It allows you to expand operations without compromising on performance or quality. If scalability is not planned, a business may suffer from its own success, collapsing under the strain of increased customer demands on an inadequate infrastructure.

1. Cloud Computing

- **Flexibility and Scalability**: Cloud computing services like Amazon Web Services (AWS), Google Cloud Platform (GCP), and Microsoft Azure offer flexible and scalable solutions that can grow with your business. These platforms allow you to scale resources up or down based on demand, ensuring that you only pay for what you use.
- **Disaster Recovery and Security**: Cloud services provide robust security features and disaster recovery options, protecting your data and ensuring business continuity.

2. Scalable Software Solutions

- **Modular Software**: Invest in modular software solutions

that can be easily expanded as your business grows. This includes customer relationship management (CRM) systems, enterprise resource planning (ERP) software, and other business applications.
- **Automation Tools**: Implement automation tools to streamline repetitive tasks and improve efficiency. Tools like Zapier, UiPath, and Blue Prism can automate processes across various business functions, reducing manual effort and minimizing errors.

3. Scalable Network Infrastructure

- **Network Design**: Design your network infrastructure to support scalability. This includes using scalable networking equipment, optimizing bandwidth usage, and ensuring redundancy to handle increased traffic.
- **Content Delivery Networks (CDNs)**: Utilize CDNs to distribute content efficiently to users around the globe. CDNs help reduce latency and improve the performance of your online services, providing a better user experience.

Developing Robust Processes

Robust processes are essential for maintaining quality and efficiency as you scale. Well-defined processes ensure consistency, reduce errors, and improve overall productivity.

1. Standard Operating Procedures (SOPs)

- **Documentation**: Create detailed SOPs for all critical business processes. These documents should outline step-by-step instructions for performing tasks, ensuring that everyone follows the same procedures.
- **Training and Onboarding**: Use SOPs as a foundation for training and onboarding new employees. Well-documented processes help new hires get up to speed quickly and perform their roles effectively.

2. Process Optimization

- **Continuous Improvement**: Regularly review and optimize your processes to identify inefficiencies and areas for improvement. Implement lean methodologies and Six Sigma principles to enhance process efficiency and reduce waste.
- **Performance Metrics**: Establish key performance indicators (KPIs) to measure the effectiveness of your processes. Use these metrics to track performance, identify bottlenecks, and make data-driven decisions.

3. Quality Control

- **Quality Assurance (QA)**: Implement QA processes to ensure that products and services meet high standards of quality. This includes regular inspections, testing, and audits.
- **Feedback Loops**: Establish feedback loops to gather input from employees and customers. Use this feedback to identify issues, make improvements, and ensure that quality standards are maintained.

In scaling your business you may need to bring on more recruits. Remember the ideas from chapter 5. Do not compromise on the quality of employee when hiring in large numbers.

Scaling Strategies for Different Business Functions

1. Scaling Production and Manufacturing

- **Outsourcing and Partnerships**: Consider outsourcing certain production processes or forming partnerships with manufacturers to increase capacity without significant capital investment.
- **Lean Manufacturing**: Implement lean manufacturing principles to optimize production processes, reduce waste, and improve efficiency.

2. Scaling Sales and Marketing

- **Sales Automation**: Use sales automation tools to streamline

sales processes, manage leads, and improve customer relationship management.
- **Digital Marketing**: Invest in digital marketing strategies to reach a larger audience. This includes search engine optimization (SEO), pay-per-click (PPC) advertising, social media marketing, and content marketing.

3. Scaling Customer Support

- **Customer Support Software**: Implement customer support software like Zendesk, Freshdesk, or Intercom to manage customer inquiries efficiently and provide timely support.
- **Self-Service Options**: Develop self-service options such as FAQs, knowledge bases, and chatbots to help customers find answers to common questions quickly.

Case Study: Amazon's Efficient Scaling

Amazon's journey from an online bookstore to a global e-commerce giant exemplifies efficient scaling.

Scalable Infrastructure

- **Cloud Computing**: Amazon Web Services (AWS) provides the scalable infrastructure that supports Amazon's massive e-commerce platform and many other businesses worldwide.
- **Fulfillment Centers**: Amazon's extensive network of fulfillment centers is designed to scale efficiently, allowing the company to handle increasing volumes of orders and deliver products quickly.

Robust Processes

- **Standardized Procedures**: Amazon's operations are driven by standardized procedures that ensure consistency and efficiency across its global network.
- **Continuous Improvement**: Amazon continuously optimizes its processes through data-driven decision-making and innovation.

Talent and Culture

- **Customer-Centric Culture**: Amazon's culture of customer obsession drives its focus on delivering value and maintaining high standards of quality.
- **Employee Development**: Amazon invests in employee development through training programs and clear career paths, ensuring that its workforce is equipped to support growth.

Implementing Efficient Scaling in Your Startup

To scale operations efficiently in your startup, follow these steps:

1. **Invest in Scalable Infrastructure**: Use cloud computing, scalable software, and robust network infrastructure to support growth.
2. **Develop Robust Processes**: Create and optimize SOPs, implement QA processes, and establish performance metrics.
3. **Build the Right Team**: Recruit strategically, develop employees, and foster a positive work culture.
4. **Scale Business Functions**: Use outsourcing, sales automation, digital marketing, and customer support software to scale production, sales, and customer support.

Chapter Recap

Scaling operations efficiently is essential for sustaining growth and maintaining quality in a rapidly expanding business. By investing in scalable infrastructure, developing robust processes, and building the right team, you can ensure that your business can handle increased demand without compromising on performance or customer satisfaction. As you continue to implement the principles of Blitzkrieg in your business, remember that efficient scaling is about expanding your capabilities while preserving the agility and value that drive your success.

CHAPTER 9: RISK MANAGEMENT AND CONTINGENCY PLANNING

In a fast-paced business environment, the ability to identify, assess, and mitigate risks is crucial for sustained success. Effective risk management and contingency planning ensure that a business can navigate uncertainties, minimize potential damages, and maintain operational continuity. This chapter explores the importance of risk management and provides frameworks for developing robust risk management and contingency plans.

The Importance of Risk Management

1. **Preserving Business Continuity**: Effective risk management ensures that your business can continue to operate smoothly even when unexpected events occur.
2. **Protecting Assets**: Identifying and mitigating risks helps protect your physical, financial, and intellectual assets from potential threats.
3. **Enhancing Decision-Making**: Understanding potential risks allows for more informed decision-making, ensuring that strategies are resilient and adaptable.
4. **Building Stakeholder Confidence**: Demonstrating a proactive approach to risk management builds confidence among investors, customers, and employees, reinforcing trust and stability.

Identifying and Assessing Risks

1. Risk Identification

The first step in risk management is identifying potential risks that could impact your business. This involves considering various categories of risks, including:

- **Operational Risks**: Risks related to day-to-day operations,

such as equipment failures, supply chain disruptions, or human errors.
- **Financial Risks**: Risks related to financial performance, including market fluctuations, credit risks, and liquidity issues.
- **Strategic Risks**: Risks arising from strategic decisions, such as entering new markets, launching new products, or changes in industry regulations.
- **Reputational Risks**: Risks that could damage your brand and reputation, such as negative publicity, product recalls, or customer dissatisfaction.
- **Compliance Risks**: Risks related to non-compliance with laws, regulations, and industry standards.

2. Risk Assessment

Once potential risks are identified, assess their likelihood and impact to prioritize them effectively. This involves:

- **Likelihood**: Evaluating the probability of each risk occurring. This can be categorized as low, medium, or high.
- **Impact**: Assessing the potential consequences of each risk on your business. This can also be categorized as low, medium, or high.

Mitigating Risks

After identifying and assessing risks, the next step is to develop strategies to mitigate them. This involves:

1. Risk Avoidance

- **Decision-Making**: Avoid high-risk activities or decisions that could expose your business to significant threats. For example, avoid entering volatile markets without thorough research and preparation.

2. Risk Reduction

- **Preventive Measures**: Implement measures to reduce

the likelihood or impact of risks. This might include regular maintenance of equipment, diversifying suppliers, or investing in employee training.
- **Quality Control**: Establish robust quality control processes to detect and address issues before they escalate.

3. Risk Transfer

- **Insurance**: Transfer risks to third parties through insurance policies. This can include property insurance, liability insurance, and business interruption insurance.
- **Outsourcing**: Outsource high-risk activities to specialized providers who can manage them more effectively.

4. Risk Acceptance

- **Contingency Planning**: Accept certain risks that cannot be avoided, reduced, or transferred, and develop contingency plans to manage their impact if they occur.

Developing Effective Contingency Plans

Contingency planning involves preparing for potential risks and ensuring that your business can respond effectively if they materialize.

1. Scenario Analysis

- **Identify Scenarios**: Identify potential risk scenarios that could impact your business. These scenarios should cover a range of possibilities, from minor disruptions to major crises.
- **Develop Response Plans**: For each scenario, develop detailed response plans outlining the steps to be taken to manage the situation. This should include roles and responsibilities, communication strategies, and resource requirements.

2. Business Continuity Planning

- **Essential Functions**: Identify essential business functions that must be maintained during a disruption. This includes

critical operations, services, and processes.
- **Backup Systems**: Establish backup systems and processes to ensure that essential functions can continue. This might include backup power supplies, alternative work locations, and data redundancy.

3. Communication Plans

- **Internal Communication**: Develop communication plans to ensure that employees are informed and aware of their roles and responsibilities during a crisis.
- **External Communication**: Prepare communication strategies for external stakeholders, including customers, suppliers, and the media. Clear and transparent communication is essential for maintaining trust and managing reputational risks.

4. Regular Testing and Review

- **Drills and Simulations**: Conduct regular drills and simulations to test the effectiveness of your contingency plans. This helps identify gaps and areas for improvement.
- **Continuous Improvement**: Regularly review and update your risk management and contingency plans based on feedback, new information, and changing circumstances.

Case Study: Toyota's Risk Management and Contingency Planning

Toyota's approach to risk management and contingency planning provides a valuable example of best practices.

Identifying and Assessing Risks

- **Comprehensive Risk Identification**: Toyota identifies a wide range of risks, including operational, financial, strategic, reputational, and compliance risks.
- **Thorough Risk Assessment**: The company assesses the likelihood and impact of each risk, prioritizing those that

could significantly affect its operations and reputation.

Mitigating Risks

- **Supply Chain Diversification**: Toyota reduces supply chain risks by diversifying its suppliers and maintaining strong relationships with multiple vendors.
- **Quality Control**: The company implements rigorous quality control measures to detect and address issues early, reducing the likelihood of product recalls and reputational damage.

Developing Contingency Plans

- **Scenario Analysis**: Toyota conducts scenario analysis to prepare for potential disruptions, such as natural disasters, economic downturns, and supply chain interruptions.
- **Business Continuity Planning**: The company identifies essential functions and establishes backup systems to ensure continuity. This includes maintaining buffer stock and alternative production sites.
- **Communication Plans**: Toyota has clear communication plans for both internal and external stakeholders, ensuring transparency and trust during crises.
- **Regular Testing and Review**: The company conducts regular drills and continuously improves its risk management and contingency plans based on feedback and new information.

Implementing Risk Management and Contingency Planning in Your Startup

To implement effective risk management and contingency planning in your startup, follow these steps:

1. **Identify and Assess Risks**: Conduct a comprehensive risk identification and assessment process to prioritize potential threats.
2. **Develop Mitigation Strategies**: Implement strategies to avoid, reduce, transfer, or accept risks based on their likelihood and impact.

3. **Create Contingency Plans**: Develop detailed contingency plans for potential risk scenarios, ensuring business continuity and clear communication.
4. **Test and Review**: Regularly test your contingency plans through drills and simulations, and continuously improve them based on feedback and new information.

Chapter Recap

Risk management and contingency planning are essential components of a successful business strategy. By proactively identifying, assessing, and mitigating risks, and developing robust contingency plans, your business can navigate uncertainties and maintain operational continuity. As you continue to implement the principles of Blitzkrieg in your business, remember that effective risk management is about being prepared for the unexpected and ensuring that your business can adapt and thrive in a dynamic environment.

CHAPTER 10: LEADERSHIP IN A BLITZKRIEG BUSINESS

In a high-speed, high-stakes business environment, effective leadership is crucial for driving success and achieving extraordinary results. The Blitzkrieg approach to business requires leaders who can inspire, motivate, and guide their teams with agility, decisiveness, and vision. This chapter examines the qualities and skills required for effective leadership in a fast-paced business setting and provides practical strategies for leaders to empower their teams and foster a culture of excellence.

Essential Qualities of Effective Leaders

1. Visionary Thinking

- **Strategic Vision**: Effective leaders have a clear and compelling vision for the future of the business. They can articulate long-term goals and strategies that inspire and guide their teams.
- **Forward-Looking**: Visionary leaders anticipate market trends, technological advancements, and potential disruptions, positioning their businesses to capitalize on opportunities and mitigate risks.

2. Decisiveness

- **Quick Decision-Making**: In a fast-paced environment, leaders must make timely decisions with confidence. They gather relevant information, weigh options, and choose the best course of action without unnecessary delay.
- **Risk Management**: Decisive leaders understand the importance of balancing speed with calculated risk-taking. They are willing to take bold actions while considering potential impacts and contingency plans.

3. Agility and Adaptability

- **Flexibility**: Effective leaders are adaptable and open to change. They can pivot strategies and adjust plans in response to evolving market conditions and new information.
- **Continuous Learning**: Agile leaders embrace continuous learning and improvement. They stay updated on industry trends and best practices, fostering a culture of innovation within their teams.

4. Emotional Intelligence

- **Empathy**: Leaders with high emotional intelligence understand and empathize with their team members' needs, concerns, and motivations. This fosters a supportive and collaborative work environment.
- **Self-Awareness**: Emotionally intelligent leaders are self-aware, recognizing their strengths and weaknesses. They use this awareness to build strong relationships and lead with authenticity.

5. Inspirational Motivation

- **Passion and Enthusiasm**: Inspirational leaders are passionate about their vision and mission. Their enthusiasm is contagious, motivating their teams to strive for excellence and overcome challenges.
- **Empowerment**: Effective leaders empower their teams by providing the resources, support, and autonomy needed to succeed. They trust their team members to take ownership and make decisions.

Skills for Leading in a High-Speed Environment

1. Communication

- **Clarity**: Clear and concise communication is essential for aligning teams and ensuring everyone understands the goals, expectations, and priorities. Leaders should articulate their vision and strategies effectively.

- **Active Listening**: Leaders must actively listen to their team members, valuing their input and feedback. This fosters a culture of open communication and mutual respect.

2. Delegation

- **Empowering Teams**: Delegation involves trusting team members with responsibilities and decision-making authority. Effective leaders delegate tasks based on individuals' strengths and expertise.
- **Accountability**: While delegating, leaders must also establish accountability. They set clear expectations and monitor progress, providing guidance and support as needed.

3. Conflict Resolution

- **Mediating Disputes**: In a fast-paced environment, conflicts can arise. Effective leaders mediate disputes and address issues promptly, ensuring that conflicts are resolved constructively.
- **Promoting Collaboration**: Leaders foster a collaborative culture where team members work together towards common goals, reducing the likelihood of conflicts and enhancing overall productivity.

4. Strategic Thinking

- **Big-Picture Perspective**: Strategic thinking involves understanding the broader context and long-term implications of decisions. Leaders must balance immediate needs with future goals.
- **Analytical Skills**: Effective leaders analyze data, trends, and market conditions to inform their strategies. They use critical thinking to evaluate options and make informed decisions.

Inspiring and Motivating Teams

1. Setting Clear Goals

- **SMART Goals**: Leaders set Specific, Measurable, Achievable, Relevant, and Time-bound (SMART) goals that provide direction and focus. Clear goals help teams understand what is expected and how success will be measured.
- **Alignment**: Ensure that individual and team goals align with the overall business objectives. This creates a sense of purpose and unity within the organization.

2. Recognizing and Rewarding Achievement

- **Recognition Programs**: Implement recognition programs to celebrate individual and team achievements. Public recognition boosts morale and motivates employees to maintain high performance.
- **Incentives**: Offer incentives, such as bonuses, promotions, and professional development opportunities, to reward outstanding performance and encourage continuous improvement.

3. Providing Development Opportunities

- **Training and Education**: Invest in training and education programs to enhance employees' skills and knowledge. This demonstrates a commitment to their growth and development.
- **Career Pathing**: Provide clear career paths and opportunities for advancement within the organization. This motivates employees to perform at their best and stay with the company long-term.

Case Study: Leadership at Tesla

Tesla's leadership, under the direction of Elon Musk, exemplifies many of the qualities and skills required for effective leadership in a high-speed business environment.

Visionary Thinking

- **Bold Vision**: Elon Musk's vision for Tesla includes

accelerating the world's transition to sustainable energy. This clear and compelling vision inspires employees and stakeholders alike.
- **Innovation**: Musk anticipates market trends and drives innovation, positioning Tesla as a leader in electric vehicles and renewable energy solutions.

Decisiveness and Agility

- **Rapid Decision-Making**: Tesla's leadership is known for making swift decisions, enabling the company to stay ahead of competitors and adapt to market changes quickly.
- **Adaptability**: The company continuously evolves its strategies and product offerings based on market feedback and technological advancements.

Inspirational Motivation

- **Passion**: Musk's passion for sustainable energy and technological innovation motivates his team to push the boundaries of what is possible.
- **Empowerment**: Tesla's leadership empowers employees by fostering a culture of creativity and autonomy, encouraging them to take risks and innovate.

Implementing Effective Leadership in Your Startup

To implement effective leadership in your startup, consider these steps:

1. **Articulate a Clear Vision**: Develop and communicate a compelling vision that aligns with your business goals and inspires your team.
2. **Foster Decisiveness and Agility**: Encourage quick decision-making and adaptability within your leadership team. Embrace continuous learning and improvement.
3. **Enhance Emotional Intelligence**: Develop empathy, self-awareness, and strong interpersonal skills to build a

supportive and collaborative work environment.
4. **Set Clear Goals and Recognize Achievements**: Establish SMART goals, recognize and reward achievements, and provide development opportunities to motivate your team.
5. **Promote Open Communication and Collaboration**: Maintain open lines of communication, actively listen to your team, and foster a culture of collaboration and mutual respect.

Conclusion

Effective leadership is the cornerstone of success in a high-speed, high-stakes business environment. By embodying qualities such as visionary thinking, decisiveness, agility, emotional intelligence, and inspirational motivation, leaders can guide their teams to achieve extraordinary results. As you continue to implement the principles of Blitzkrieg in your business, remember that leadership is about inspiring, motivating, and empowering your team to navigate challenges and seize opportunities with confidence and resilience.

CHAPTER 11: CONCLUSION – THE PATH TO SUSTAINED SUCCESS

As we draw this journey to a close, let's recap the core principles and strategies covered in "Blitzkrieg in Business." Throughout this book, we've explored how the principles of Blitzkrieg—speed, concentration of force, flexibility, and decisive action—can be applied to achieve breakthrough success in the business world. These principles, when thoughtfully implemented, can help any business, whether a startup or an established corporation, navigate the complex and dynamic landscape of modern markets.

The Essence of Blitzkrieg

We began by understanding the historical roots of Blitzkrieg, a military strategy that emphasized rapid, concentrated attacks to quickly overwhelm the enemy. Translating these principles to business, we identified the core tenets:

- **Speed**: Moving swiftly to outpace competitors and seize opportunities.
- **Concentration of Force**: Focusing resources on high-impact areas.
- **Flexibility**: Adapting to changes and pivoting when necessary.

Speed – The Need for Speed

In Chapter 2, we delved into the importance of speed in business. We discussed how being first to market can secure a competitive advantage and how a culture of agility can be cultivated within an organization. Key strategies included:

- Empowering employees to make quick decisions.
- Encouraging experimentation and innovation.

- Leveraging technology to automate tasks and enhance efficiency.

Concentration of Force – Focus Your Efforts

Chapter 3 emphasized the importance of concentrating resources on critical points. By focusing on high-potential opportunities and investing heavily in them, businesses can achieve significant impact. We covered:

- Analyzing the business landscape to identify key opportunities.
- Prioritizing initiatives based on potential impact and feasibility.
- Allocating resources strategically and maintaining focus on core competencies.

Flexibility – Adapting to Change

In Chapter 4, we explored the power of pivoting and the need for continuous learning and innovation. Flexibility allows businesses to respond effectively to new information and changing circumstances. Essential practices included:

- Monitoring performance and gathering customer feedback.
- Building agile teams and fostering a culture of innovation.
- Conducting regular market and competitive analysis to stay informed.

Recruitment – Building a High-Performing Team

Chapter 5 highlighted the critical role of recruitment in building a successful business. Competent employees are the backbone of any organization. We discussed:

- Defining the ideal candidate profile and utilizing multiple recruitment channels.
- Implementing a rigorous selection process and focusing on cultural fit.
- Onboarding and integrating new hires effectively while

ensuring continuous development and retention.

Balancing Speed and Value – Avoiding the Pitfalls of Rapid Execution

In Chapter 6, we addressed the challenge of maintaining value while executing quickly. Rapid execution must not come at the expense of quality. Strategies for balancing speed and value included:

- Prioritizing core features and functionality.
- Implementing robust quality assurance processes.
- Fostering a culture of excellence and efficient resource allocation.

The Power of the Minimum Viable Product (MVP)

Chapter 7 introduced the concept of the MVP as a tool for launching products quickly while ensuring they deliver significant value. We covered:

- Focusing on core features and concentrating resources on development.
- Using agile methodologies to iterate rapidly.
- Gathering and analyzing user feedback to refine the product.

Scaling Operations Efficiently

In Chapter 8, we explored strategies for scaling operations while maintaining quality and efficiency. Essential components of efficient scaling included:

- Investing in scalable infrastructure and software solutions.
- Developing robust processes and quality control measures.
- Building the right team and fostering a positive work culture.

Risk Management and Contingency Planning

Chapter 9 emphasized the importance of identifying, assessing, and mitigating risks. Effective risk management and contingency planning ensure business continuity. Key steps included:

- Conducting comprehensive risk identification and assessment.
- Developing mitigation strategies and contingency plans.
- Regularly testing and reviewing plans to ensure preparedness.

Leadership in a Blitzkrieg Business

In Chapter 10, we examined the qualities and skills required for effective leadership in a high-speed, high-stakes environment. Effective leaders inspire, motivate, and guide their teams. We highlighted:

- The importance of visionary thinking and decisiveness.
- The need for agility, adaptability, and emotional intelligence.
- Strategies for setting clear goals, recognizing achievements, and providing development opportunities.

The Path to Sustained Success

Implementing the principles of Blitzkrieg in business requires a fundamental shift in mindset and strategy. It's about moving quickly, focusing efforts, adapting to change, and leading with decisiveness. By embracing these principles, businesses can navigate the complexities of the modern market, seize opportunities, and achieve long-term success.

As you move forward, remember that the journey doesn't end here. Continuous learning, adaptation, and improvement are crucial for sustained success. Keep pushing the boundaries, stay agile, and lead with confidence. The principles of Blitzkrieg are not just about winning battles but about building a resilient and thriving business capable of enduring and prospering in an ever-changing world.

www.ingramcontent.com/pod-product-compliance
Lightning Source LLC
Chambersburg PA
CBHW072000210526
45479CB00003B/1007